Crystals of Light

To Flo,
Good Luck!

Robert F. Newman

Crystals of Light

by

Robert L. Neumann

DORRANCE PUBLISHING CO., INC.
PITTSBURGH, PENNSYLVANIA 15222

ISBN # 0-8059-3776-5
Printed in the United States of America

First Printing

For information or to order additional books, please write:
Dorrance Publishing Co., Inc.
643 Smithfield Street
Pittsburgh, Pennsylvania 15222
U.S.A.

Contents

Forbear

In the black night
The white wind chimes
Sing
As the breeze precedes
Webs of snow.

A Beginning

Through a galaxy of the ages
A space window
Shows the birth of a planet
In the blue shades of love.

Silence

The silence of the dark night
Is deafening to the ears.

Devotional

It is the secret wish that
Makes a life whole
Or is it hard toil
From year through year?
Perhaps it is the love
Of His creation
The trees in the rain
The sand in the storm
The sun in the calm
And forever the love
Of fellow man and civilization
As it comes out of its
Sleep and into the light
Of His peace.

Christmas Eve

A Northern wind
The evergreen trees,
A midnight snowfall
Greets this Christmas Eve
The birth of our dear Lord.

Belief

Sharing future space
With a world that believes in
The birds' early morning call,
A snowfall at midnight,
A warm rain on a spring day,
And the pink blossoms
Of flowers in summertime.

Spirit

The cold mountain air
Chills the icicles
Fastened to the gray rocks.
The snow at the peak
Will not melt in the spring,
The clear atmosphere
On the mountain top
Is brilliant in the sun's rays.
From this spot one
Can talk to God.
Summer, winter, spring, fall
Is the ageless reply.

Nature's Melodies

The music of the wind
Cascades down the canyon walls
And touches a note of
Playful melody in the
Sparkling river.
A symphony of brilliance
Played on a bed of sand.

Side by Side

Traveling through space
Gravity holding us in
This plane.
After traveling a thousand
Roads, I will walk
Beside you through valleys
Of darkness to mountains
Of light, never to stray
From my undying love and
Devotion for you.

Compassions

To be at ease
And reminiscing through all
The lost and forgotten
With good friends,
Good talk, coffee,
And traveling through
The structure of a lifetime
Begun and made whole.

Morning

In the moment before dawn
In the deep stillness of the night
A crack of light breaks the
Blackness,
And this morning is entering
Its space on this planet.

Metaphors

The flame is eternal
The evergreens ring the circle
And are everlasting.
A Christmas candle
Sits in its wreath holder
On the dining room
Table at dawn.

Universal

The wind's rapture
Plays a lonely melody
Rising from the valley
Hidden between the hills
But are we alone?
We are joined by the stars,
The sun, the moon, the
Sparkling streams, the cold
Sea, and are cradled in
Creation to always
Enter the living calm
Of our Lord's peace and love.

Complete

To follow what is real
Is a righteous path.
To recognize the fantasy is
The sign of a healthy mind.
To become a whole person
Is the task of the hour.

Wild Fowl

Soft as an angel's breath
Is the swan's flight.
As the first dawning of spring
She heads for the
Marshlands, where, hidden
In the reeds she
Makes her nest for to
Lay her eggs.
A jewel in the water by day
She hides under the black
Coat of night.
In this way, deep in her nature
She survives to raise her
Family and to live another
Spring.

Remnants

The wind hisses among the
Barren trees.
The white moon peaks from
Drifting snow-capped
Night clouds.
The last tales of winter
Are told by the clear, warm
February night.
Spring has planted its seed
Here and yet may hide.

The Way

On a lonely, long forgotten
Point of the shore
The decaying lighthouse
Is an anachronism as a
Beacon of light to the high
Seas.
Now the foghorns moan
On this foggy night
And guide the mighty
Ships through the arms
Of the sea.
The point of light
Replaced by a low groan for all
Seafarers to hear.
This music sweet to the
Ears of many days spent
On the massive, high seas.

Turn, Turn

The white and pink blossoms
Break through the amber earth
And peek out of the patch
Of snow.
These buds are living
Harbingers of spring when
The winter chill turns
To the warmth of spring.

One

We are individuals
Joined in a communion
Of the longing for
God's peace and love
Entering on the threshold
Of a universe which
Opens its arms
As the sun rises
In our desires.

Forest Tale

The white birch
Was entwined by the
Bittersweet vines
That late fall morning
As the sun caressed
The woodlands
The small peeps of the
Snow birds were heard
Among the silver-frosted
Evergreens,
Hidden for warmth over
The cold nights their
Melodies can move even
The sleeping creatures of the
Forest. The animals awake
For to survive another day.

Passing Time

The Earth is a
Haven for life.
This celestial globe
Can turn night into day
Winter to spring to summer
To fall.
The seasons pass so quickly
In this timeless universe
They seem to be playing
A melody as part of
An overall symphony of
Our Creator's destiny.

Within peace freedom exists.

Limits

The river's strength lies
Within its banks
Just as our strength
Lies within our limits.
Breaking the banks
The river becomes out of control
As breaking our
Limits leads to loss of self-control.

Quenching the Thirst

Water, the source of the
Universe.
It sustains life
It refreshes the body and spirit
It is in harmony with nature
In the form of a waterfall,
In lake, the seas, and the
Rain.
It is a gift of the Lord
To fill the weary soul.

Hunters

The evening Seminole sky
Was washed in pale yellow
And bright orange
As the sun set behind
The black rock canyon walls.
The coyote far in the distance
Sang a haunting melody
And the eagles perched
High on the cliffs
Prepared for another moonlit
Night.

Love's Will

A bit of love
Can create a
Bead of stardust
In the black pitch
Of the sky.
By His handiwork
This emotion can
Carry us from despair
From loneliness
From worthlessness
To sing the
Natural order of heavens
Droplets of love grow
In the sunshine of happiness.

Godly Ways

These words come
As straight as the tall
Pines in the northern forest.
Take care of this precious
Life you have been given
Love the ways of your dear
Lord.
Be gentle in your ways
And think of our creator
In your dreams.

Inward Bound

Look inside
For roads of many directions.
Love lies hidden in the
Inlet of the bays of the
Mind,
Waiting to express the
Spirit of the ages in a
World where one can
Travel many miles and
Yet not reach his
Destination.
Home is found in the soul.

Listen

The Lord is alive.
He speaks to us on the wind,
He speaks to us in the
Deep of a black night,
He speaks to us in the
Chorus of the birds' warbles,
He speaks to us in the roar
Of the sea.
His presence is real and
His devotion is eternal.
Good Lord, take my life
In your loving ways
And teach me the prophets'
Essences.
Buried deep in the well
Of eternal life your soul
Is divine in existence
And a natural part of
His creation.

Nature's Songs

Wide-open spaces
And midnight shores.
I sing praises to the
Life in these places.
The creatures of the prairies,
The birds of the canyon
Walls
The fish of the dark sea.
Home is the earth this
Life exists in and all
Paths roam to and from
Thoughts of these
Earthly abodes.

Little Song

Deep in the forest
Hidden among the rocks
Of a crystal brook
The sweet warbling
Of a tiny bird can
Wake even the sleeping
Thunder.

A Prayer

Each of us has
Some good and evil in him
From birth.
Do not let evil take seed.
Let good grow in love's
Garden and flowers
You sow will shine in
The light of day and night
Ever to proclaim a victory
Over evils' appetite and
Live in the Lord's kingdom
Here on earth.

A Seed

Hope shines eternal
As a beacon of prayers.
The prayers are the light
That hope and love
Live hand in hand.
Everyone hopes to love
And His love
Grows in us all.

Growing

As you grow
Let your love show.
It can turn cloudy skies
Into bright sunshine
A tear of sorrow
Into laughs of joy,
A bitter pain into
A great healing
But above all it fulfills
The spirit
Its creator designed.

Day by Day

It's midnight here at home
You can feel the bones
Of the old day pass into
Dust.
And the midnight moon
Shines through black leaves
Making haunting
Measures in the
Fields below.
Soon the bright moon
Will yield to a rising
Orange sun and the
Full circle of another day's
Dance of life will begin.

A Cradle Song

A lullaby calms the fears
Of a frightened child
Just as the soft breezes
Of a spring morning
Caresses the melted dew on
The tiny flowering buds
In the bright sunshine.

Roads

The rays of moonbeams
Light the trail to guide
A cowboy home and
A lost ship to return
To port.
This light touches the earth
In a natural way of belonging.

Globe

Bright, fire-falls of
Sunlight brighten this
Lonely island.
This brilliant lamp of energy
Not only toasts the beaches
But warms the cool waters.
It helps make crops grow
And stands as the
Life-giver of our galaxy.

Passing Passage

The seasons turn
Colors of green, red, brown,
And white.
The brown ashes fall
Becoming a brilliant white
Of an icy winter.
The spring brings eternal
Green in new life
And the red sunsets of
A summer sky
Complete the cycle.

In a Life

As a new star is
Born and shines
And falls eternally
In deep space
We are born to shine
As our souls in the
New day of His creation.
We also fall in the
End, but to pass
Through this life
In completeness is in
Itself beautiful to believe.

A Conversation

Sharing an idea,
Arriving at a conclusion,
Reaching deep into the soul
For meaning,
These experiences can
Give you the wisdom
Of the stars
And satisfaction of a
Lifetime.

Forever

Making a statement
In a musical
Form strikes a universal life
Pulse
Just as nature washes the
Mountains with snow
And rain to the tune
Of a willful, pulsating
Wind.

A Year

The snow peaks are
Melting now that it is
Late summer.
An unusually heavy
Rainfall gushes the mountain
Stream with cold, icy
Water and the leaves
On the trees lay heavy.

Fulfillment

Make all that you love
In this life a part of you
Then you can call on the
Spirit of life to fill the
Deepest pool of love
And reach out to the
Point of overflowing kindness.

Praise

In a deep mountain glade
The rock monastery exists.
From the icy spring
The well is visited daily by the
Brothers of purpose.
And their purpose is to
Lead the simple life and
Worship routines daily.
They make their rounds beneath
The cracking chapel bells.
The swallows rest on their
Shoulders just as the
Love of God rests in their
Souls, full of devotion
They sing crystals of praise.

Home

Back in the mountain hills
Again.
With the wind at the fore
I enter a clearing and
Taste the wild berries the
Birds have left.
Farther down the wooded
Peak lies a glacial lake
With its water an icy blue.
After a dip I sit by the
Campfire over a hot cup
Of coffee and meditate
On the stars and the creation.

Folklore

My Indian friend
Had the patience of
A sturdy birch in
A prairie wind
As he molded his craft.
He bent with the fissures
Of the new clay on
The wheel.
His fingers were so deft
They seemed to be a part
Of his creation.
And in the distance
The wind fowl of the
Forest sang his
Quiet tune time.

A Visit

Roaming the farmland
Pastures and green meadows
Golden fields of tall grass
Here, under an old dying
Tree are wild strawberries
Showing their crimson colors.
There, in a wild overgrown
Clump of bushes, the
Raspberries show their goodness
Hidden in thick foliage.
And now is the time to
Visit the immortal elm
Tree and share the bounty
Of this year's crops in a
Picnic under the spreading
Branches.
To visit in my memory the
Roaming fields is the
Choice of a pastime gone by.

Ancient Way

The old rusty cross
With the palm branches
At the top was discovered
Underneath a wooden vessel
Deep in the forest.
With further dig in the
Sandy, musty soil
A subterranean stream burst
Through the earth.
To remind mankind that
The river of life flows eternally
In our lives, and always
Ends at the beginning.

A Day

Have you ever heard
The night fall
On a black, iron, starry night
Among the whistling wind
Blowing drifts of snow by
The wayside?
The night falls
Only to hear the dawn
Break on a new, fresh
Snow land captured only by
The atmosphere of this earth,
And warmed by the star-shine
Of the sun.

A Call

Come in out of the cold
Mankind,
And sit by the fire that
Began your civilization,
A long, long time ago.
And share in the warmth
Of friendship that comes
From the soul.
God has given us this
Radiance to share equally
Among all and to bring
This earth to bring to the
Garden, where the leaves
On the trees are as
Numerous as the family
Of man and the flowers
Are jewels of all of us planted
Deep in His soul.

Sea Angel

She was born of the golden sand
And she knew the water
As well as the wind.
Love was to her as a
Moth is to the flame.
And one fine day
She left the cold of the day's winter
And appeared
In the fire of a sunny
Day, kissing the ground
That held her and
Praying for the love
That made her whole.
She had come into the
World as an angel of God
And as a forbearer of things
To pass.

Breaking Through

The little path in the woods
Was filled with old forgotten
Leaves, dirt, branches,
And every once in a while
On the left and right
Small patches of snow.
Walking one would hear
A sparrow or snow bird
Peep from some hidden
Evergreen.
It was warm that day
And you could smell
Spring in the air.
The winter's night has begun
Yielding to a springtime
Day.

Memories

The gurgling and clucking
Of the chickens in the coop
Digging for grubs.
The grunts of the old sow
In the pig pen.
The fresh smell of hay in
The hayloft.
The whines of the horses
In the fields.
The mooing of cattle in
The meadow.
These are sounds of rural
America and farms,
Sounds of my childhood,
Days which follow me
Through my life.
Oh! To return to the
Golden days were one
Could drink cold, fresh
Water from the streams.
Lay in the sunlight of
High meadow grass and
Look in the deep, blue sky.
Walk in the clean, sparkling
Air, and ramble thorough
Forest paths.
For a lifetime these feelings
Of hand in hand with
Nature are uplifting as
The Lord's creation
Which made all possible.

Conquest

At the foot of the mountain
The task seemed ominous.
Through thickets of brambles
And foliage
He climbed.
Reaching the snow line the
Trees were burdened with
White powdery snow.
His determination to reach
The peak transversing the canyon
Walls and passes
Was what held him together.
And at nightfall ear
A fire and in the cold
Mountain air a
Million country stars
Celebrated his arrival.

My Friend

My friend with the white
Hair and white beard
He can be pessimistic at
Times but also can be
As gentle and exact
As a veteran surgeon
With a scalpel.
His stories can hold my
Interest as told
As actually happening.
Many times over a good
Cup of coffee and many
Cigarettes we have discussed
Worldly ways.
Now looking for any answers
But just enjoying good
Discussion and each others'
Company.
Friends such as him are
As precious as jewels which
Shine brilliantly rare.

Bob

Bob plays his music with
Grace.
He is quick with a
Humorous tale
And will evoke laughter
With such.
His devotion to his close
Relationships and family
In a shining jewel
Standing alone in a
Sometime impersonal
World
And cultivated in him
Innocent desires and emotions.
Bob is a friend of mine.

John

John's heart and soul are as
Peaceful and calm as God's
Love,
His red Irish hair and face
Are as weathered and sculptured
As a fisherman's tale.
He is lean and trim.
A victim of life's misfortunes
He accepts his burdens and
Lives as you and I.
Maybe we can all learn some-
Thing from John.

Hometown Boy

Born of the wind,
He travels the streets
Of his hometown
With music in his ears
And the love of
The ages in his heart.
He works in wood
And would just as soon
Paint a morning sunrise
As well as a breaking
Storm on his carvings.
His life fell into place
Among the multitudes
And alone.
Following the teachings
Of his elders,
He learned from the past
What shines bright in
The present.
He looks at
The future with a hopeful smile.

Musing

I passed by an old
Red and brown farmhouse
With fields of wheat
Stretching to the sunrise.
I passed a group of old
Men on a back porch
Just sittin'.
I smelled the columbine
As it was in full bloom.
The foothills of the Rockies
Seemed to beg me to
Climb the summit.
The old hoot-owl
Sang in the dead of night.
I was in the heartland
Of America.

Nature's Rhyme

The wind carries the seed.
The sun comes to the call.
The rain joins in with its fall.
The amber rich soil is its
Home.
And the flower breaks free
In sweet harmony.

Reminisce

That night was
A rendezvous with the past.
Music from the old
Days on streams of memories.
Thoughts of my first love
Young at heart but old
It seemed then.
The years gone by pass
So surely and comfort
My memories hidden deeply
In the well of time.

ع.

Peace

In the temple garden
The red, blue, green, and
Purple birds hide in the
Rich, green foliage.
The peacock spreads its
Plume.
The wind makes the sound of
A low flute whistling
Through the trees.
The pools waterfalls gurgle
And splash on the brown
And gray rocks.
The peace of the garden invades
Every inch of your
Being and the soul dwells in
Harmony with the
Natural world.

Rain

Rain, it washes the sand
On the shore.
It feeds the forest,
It nourishes the seeds in
The soil to become roots
And then majestic trees.
It can be as gentle as a
Down feather.
With the mighty wind it
Can be as viscious
As the wrath of nature.
But it supplies the earth
With water
And is new life.

The River

The cold, clear, dancing
River has
Beginnings at the snow
Caps and winds
Through mountain passes
And desert canyons.
Underground it starts as
A stream
As the snow melts it
Rushes on a course
To the sea,
Through black forests
And green fields
And prairies.
It can be called a highway
From its source
To all parts of the earth.

Preacher

His skin was black
And weathered by the burden
He carried.
He talked of The Book of God
And sang of love
And peace on the street corners.
His songs spoke of his
Whole life,
A life filled with love
And hope for a better day
For mankind,
His husky voice reflected
Many a spontaneous
Sermon and he
Walked in the sun.

Becoming

We walked hand in hand
With the Milky Way
That starry night.
We left our thoughts
In a black void
In deep space
And melted into the universe.

Duality

We split the moment
Between hope and despair.
The hope came rushing
As a sparkling river rolling
Between plains of prairie
Fields.
It followed the sun.
Despair appeared as a
Raging sea-based storm
With black clouds making
The deep blue water seem
A coal black.
The mind changes so
Quickly when one is wondering
Alone.

A Day

A gentle surprise
Breaks into the lull of
Early and mid-morning sun.
The intense heat of the
Afternoon gives way
To a peaceful sunset.
Night follows on the
Moon's footsteps until
The next dawn.

Mirror

Gentle droplets of rain
Strike the clear, cool pond
In the hidden valley.
Crystals of lights send
Sparks of glistening silver
On the shimmering
Canyon walls.

Mountain Angel

Her eyes shown of a faraway
Land.
Her hair was an auburn brown,
Her voice spoke with raptures
As the wind.
She was born of the mountains
And knew the silence of an
Eagle in flight.
Her spirit would not let
Me escape.
Deep down in her is a
Part of me joined in a
Communion of love.

Passage

We rode on angel's wings
To an island eden
With His song in our souls.
The wind, the silver sand,
The lights at night
Filled our sense in that
Summer wonderland where
The sun greets the sea.
And time passed.

Living Ways

Plant your seeds in
Childhood,
Sow your crops during your
Life,
Harvest your love in the
Twilight years.

Dream Isle

The silver waves
Kissed the golden
Sands
As the frigates above
Rose the balmy trade winds.
The turquoise water
Shone
And reflected the multi-
Colored fish below.
The sun rose slowly above
The calm sea
Spreading orange and red threads through a blue sky and
A day dawned on this
Tropical retreat.

Reflection

The music carries
Through the room as
A peaceful breeze in the pines,
It has the rhythm of
A country home
And reminds us of
Island seas.
It refreshes the memory
And quiets the senses.

I Am

Do you remember me?
I was there when the first
Storm passes over the seas.
I was there when the first
Mountain erupted from the
Earth.
I was there on that sad Friday
When the clouds covered the sun.
I will be at your back and
Sometimes we will come
Face to face.
I am the wind.

Paths

It leads the insects on
Their way,
It guides the birds of the
Wild through the seasons,
It warns the animals of the
Forest of danger,
It is a guiding light in
The order of nature,
Instinct, it is the foundation
Of life.

Future

The torch of love
Beams through the iron
Black night.
The sign flashes from
nation to nation around
This weary Earth.
His love surpasses
All bitterness and hatred
And blankets the world
In an eternal season of
harmony and peace.

Prophet

From deep in the universe
The three stars
Shine with the purest light.
They formed a triangle
In the heavens
And are a sign
That peace and love
Have fallen upon this
Earth.

Country Sunday

We walked in the
Country meadow that Sunday
With a canopy of deep
Blue above dotted by
Whispers of white.
We touched the blue
Spruce Christmas trees with
Our senses.
We picked crimson, black-
Berries, and wild blueberries
Growing underfoot.
The end of the day was reached
With a swim in
The clear, cool pool.
Sundays, Sundays, there
Is no day as a late
Summer Sunday.

Robert L. Neumann

Picture

Crystals of light
Filter through the panes
Of windows in that
Northern farmhouse
Dayroom.
The green foliage of the
High fast-growing plants
Warmed the air and a
Sudden flower popped its
Brilliance from within the
Leaves.
The air was warm and sweet
As the fall sun fell
Softly on this peaceful
Place in time.